Student Interactive

myView®
LITERACY
1

SAVVAS
LEARNING COMPANY

ISBN-13: 978-0-134-90877-9

ISBN-10:　　0-134-90877-5

10　22

Julie Coiro, Ph.D.

Jim Cummins, Ph.D.

Pat Cunningham, Ph.D.

Elfrieda Hiebert, Ph.D.

Pamela Mason, Ed.D.

Ernest Morrell, Ph.D.

P. David Pearson, Ph.D.

Frank Serafini, Ph.D.

Alfred Tatum, Ph.D.

Sharon Vaughn, Ph.D.

Judy Wallis, Ed.D.

Lee Wright, Ed.D.

Imagine That

Copyright © SAVVAS Learning Company LLC. All Rights Reserved.

Essential Question

How can we use our imaginations?

▶ Watch

"Ready, Set, Imagine!" See how people use their imaginations to create things.

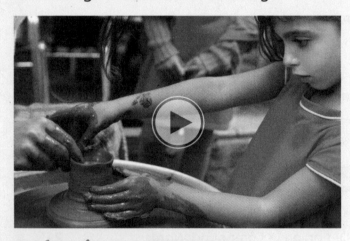

TURN and TALK How do you use your imagination?

SAVVAS
realize™

Go ONLINE for
all lessons.

▶ VIDEO

◀)) AUDIO

🎮 GAME

✎ ANNOTATE

📖 BOOK

🔍 RESEARCH

Reading-Writing Bridge

- Academic Vocabulary
- Read Like a Writer, Write for a Reader
- Spelling • Language and Conventions

Writing Workshop

Poetry

- Plan Your Poetry
- Word Choice • Rhyme
- Edit for Adverbs that Convey Time • Publish and Celebrate

Project-Based Inquiry

- Inquire • Research • Collaborate

Independent Reading

When you read independently, you read books on your own. Self-select, or choose, your own book by flipping through the book and reading some of the pages. Are they too easy? Are they too hard? Or are they just right?

Each time you read your book, try to read for longer periods of time. If you read for ten minutes yesterday, read for fifteen minutes today!

Fix-Up Strategies

Try one of these ideas if something does not make sense as you read:

- re-read the word or section.
- ask questions.
- look at the pictures.
- use what you already know.

My Reading Log

Date	Book	Pages Read	Minutes Read	My Ratings
				🙂 😐 ☹️
				🙂 😐 ☹️
				🙂 😐 ☹️
				🙂 😐 ☹️
				🙂 😐 ☹️

You may wish to use a Reader's Notebook to record and respond to your reading.

Unit Goals

In this unit, you will

- read traditional stories
- write poetry
- learn about using your imagination

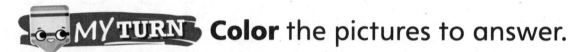 **Color** the pictures to answer.

I can read traditional stories.	👍	👎
I can make and use words to read and write about imagination.	👍	👎
I can write poetry.	👍	👎
I understand how we can use our imaginations.	👍	👎

Academic Vocabulary

create	imagine	suppose	possible

In this unit, you will learn about using your imagination. **Suppose** you want to **create** something new. Take a moment to **imagine** what is **possible.**

TURN and TALK Talk with your partner about what you can create using the materials in the picture. Which of your ideas are possible?

www.url.here

Planning Your Visit to the Zoo

Feeding Farm Animals

Grab some goodies for your favorite farm friends at the Petting Zoo. Feed is 25 cents.

Why is it important to plan ahead?

Q

Owls Up Close

Take a picture with these beautiful birds. Safety gloves are provided. Meet these feathered friends at 2:00 and 4:00 at the <u>Owlery</u>.

What does an owl sound like? Click here to find out!

Butterfly Wonderland

Add a splash of color to your day at the <u>Butterfly House</u>. Wear flowery colors to draw these fluttering beauties close. But don't touch! These animal friends are fragile.

 MY TURN (Circle) the features of this Web site, or digital text.

Segment and Blend Sounds

SEE and SAY Say each sound as you name each picture. Then blend the sounds to say each picture name again.

Digraphs wh, ch, ph, Trigraph tch

Sometimes two letters make one sound, such as **wh** in **when, ch** in **chest,** and **ph** in **graph.** These are called **digraphs.** Three letters together that make one sound, like **tch** in **hatch,** are called **trigraphs.**

MY TURN Read these words.

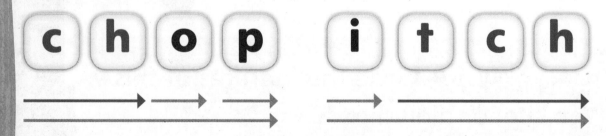

Digraphs wh, ch, ph, Trigraph tch

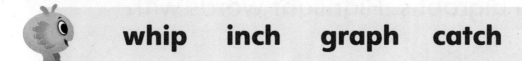 **TURN and TALK** Read these words.

| whip | inch | graph | catch |

| when | chop | lunch | hutch |

 **MY TURN** Say each picture name. Highlight the digraph or trigraph in each picture name.

ph   tch   wh

wh   ph   tch

ph   tch   wh

Digraphs wh, ch, ph, Trigraph tch

MY TURN Read the sentences. <u>Underline</u> words with digraphs. Highlight words with trigraphs.

<u>Chip</u> and <u>Phil</u> have a ball.

Patch likes to catch the ball when Chip drops it.

He chomps it and whisks by Chip.

Chip and Phil will chase Patch to get the ball.

MY TURN What happens next? Finish the story about Chip and Patch.

Chip and Patch

Segment and Blend Sounds

SEE and SAY Say each picture name. Segment the picture names into single sounds. Then blend the sounds together to say the picture names again.

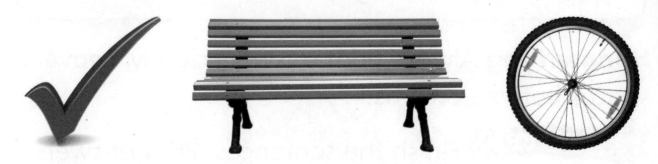

Contractions

A **contraction** is a shortened form of two words. An **apostrophe** replaces the missing letter or letters. The contraction **I'll** is the shortened form of **I** and **will**.

MY TURN Read the word pairs and the contractions. Highlight the apostrophe.

can not   can't   I am   I'm

My Words to Know

Some words you must remember and practice.

MY TURN Read these words.

no	put	good	said	round

Handwriting Always print answers clearly. Leave spaces between words.

MY TURN Finish the sentences. Print answers clearly and leave spaces between words.

1. I have a round blue rock.

2. "It is a _____ gift," I _____ .

3. Phil can _____ it in a bag.

4. One bag has _____ name on it.

Contractions

TURN and TALK Decode these contractions. Name the two words that make up each contraction.

| they'll | you're | can't |

| isn't | he's | I'm |

MY TURN Write a contraction for each word pair.

1. she will   she'll

2. has not   _____

3. we are   _____

TURN and TALK Now read each contraction. Tell your partner which letter or letters are replaced by an apostrophe.

Contractions

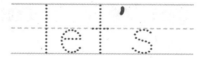 **MY TURN** Write the contraction for each word pair. Highlight the letter or letters in the word pair that are replaced by the apostrophe.

let's

1. let us

2. I will

An apostrophe can replace one or more letters.

3. she is

4. we have

 **MY TURN** Write a sentence that includes a contraction.

Can Phil Help?

Phil the Whale saw sad fish.

They can't pick a gift for Chad.

"Don't you think a shell is a good gift?" one fish said.

 AUDIO

Audio with Highlighting

 ANNOTATE

Read the story. Highlight the two **contractions.**

"Fetch the chalk," Phil said.

The fish put the chalk by Phil.

He helps sketch a round graph.

Is a shell a good gift?

Highlight the four words with the **ch** sound spelled **ch** or **tch**.

Two fish said "no."

Three fish said "yes."

<u>Phil</u> and the graph help.

Chad likes his gift!

<u>Underline</u> the two words with the
f sound spelled **ph.**

My Learning Goal I can read traditional stories.

SPOTLIGHT ON GENRE

Fable

A fable is a type of traditional story. It is a short story that teaches a moral, or lesson.

The Tortoise and the Hare

Hare asks Tortoise to race.

Problem → Hare is fast, and Tortoise is slow. During the race, Hare

Resolution → takes a nap. Tortoise passes him and wins the race. Slow

Moral → and steady wins the race.

TURN and TALK Talk about the moral of the fable.

Fable Anchor Chart

❧ A fable has ❧

★ characters that are often animals
★ a moral, or lesson
★ plot events:
  ◎ problem
  ✳ resolution, or outcome

The Ant and the Grasshopper

Preview Vocabulary

You will read these words in *The Ant and the Grasshopper*.

stored	begged	gathered	prepared

Read

Read for enjoyment.

Look at the text features, such as the title and pictures. We can use these to make a prediction, or guess, about the story. Based on text features, what can you predict?

Ask questions about the resolution, or outcome.

Talk about the moral with a partner.

Meet *the* Illustrator

Sara Rojo was born in Spain. She illustrates both English and Spanish children's books.

The Ant
and the
Grasshopper
A retelling of Aesop's fable

🔊 **AUDIO**

Audio with
Highlighting

✏ **ANNOTATE**

by Mark White
illustrated by Sara Rojo

An ant lived next to a grasshopper in a large field.

The ant woke early each summer morning.

He was a hard worker.

All day long, the ant gathered food.

He stored it in his home.

The grasshopper woke up singing every summer morning.

He had a nice voice.
He loved to make music.

All day long, he sang and danced.

"Come sing with me," the grasshopper said whenever he saw the ant.

The ant's answer was always the same.

"I can't stop now," he said.

"Not even for one song?" the grasshopper begged. "It is a lovely day!"

But the ant kept working.

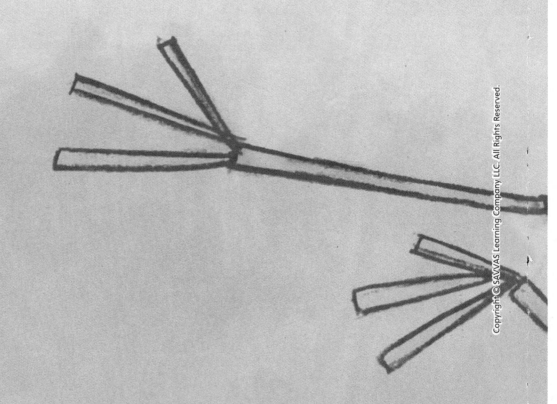

CLOSE READ

What do you predict will happen in this story? Highlight the details that make you think that.

On rainy days, the grasshopper sat around at home. He made up songs.

The ant worked at home on rainy days.

He prepared and stored his food for winter.

CLOSE READ

Highlight the details that help you correct or confirm your prediction.

One winter day, the grasshopper went to look for food.

He found nothing.

The grasshopper knocked on the ant's door.

He asked for some food.

CLOSE READ

<u>Underline</u> the grasshopper's problem.

"You spent all summer singing.
But I worked," the ant said.

"Now you can spend the
winter dancing to keep warm."

"But I know you have food," said the grasshopper.

"That's because I spent the summer getting ready for winter," the ant replied.

"There's a time for play and a time for work," the ant said.

CLOSE READ

<u>Underline</u> what the grasshopper learns from the resolution, or outcome.

Develop Vocabulary

MY TURN Write a word from the box to finish the summary of *The Ant and the Grasshopper.*

stored	begged	gathered	prepared

The ant worked hard and gathered food.

The ant _____ the food in his home.

The grasshopper _____ the ant to have fun with him.

But the ant said no.

The ant _____ for winter.

The grasshopper did not.

Check for Understanding

MY TURN Write the answers to the questions. You can look back at the text.

1. What makes this text a fable?

_____

_____

_____

2. What is the author's purpose for writing this text?

_____

_____

_____

3. What can the ant learn from the grasshopper? Use text evidence.

_____

_____

_____

Describe Plot

The **plot** is the main events in a text.
The plot can have a problem and resolution.
The **problem** is what needs to be solved.
The **resolution** is the outcome.

MY TURN What problem does the
grasshopper have? Look back at the text.

The grasshopper's problem is _____

_____

_____

What is the resolution, or outcome, of the text?

_____

_____

_____

_____

_____

Correct and Confirm Predictions

A **prediction** is what you think might happen. As you read, you can correct, or change, your prediction. After you read, you can confirm if your prediction was right. Thinking about the genre, or type of text, can help you correct and confirm predictions. In a fable, look for clues in characters' mistakes. What will they learn?

MY TURN Think about your prediction at the beginning of the text. Then write your responses. Look back at the text.

My Corrected Prediction

_____

- -

_____

- -

_____

Clue to Correct My Prediction

_____

- -

_____

Was your prediction correct?   **Yes**   **No**

Read
Together

Reflect and Share

Write to Sources

You read about a grasshopper that learns a lesson. What other characters have you read about that learn a lesson? On a separate sheet of paper, write comments about how each character learns a lesson.

Writing Comments

When writing comments about texts, it is important to use text evidence. You should:

• Find examples that support your ideas.

• Use examples from both texts.

Weekly Question

Why is it important to plan ahead?

I can make and use words to connect reading and writing.

My Learning Goal

Academic Vocabulary

Related words are connected in some way. They have similar word parts or similar meanings.

MY TURN Draw a line from each vocabulary word in the center column to its related words in the left and right columns.

creative	imagine - - - -	imagination
impossible	suppose	make
supposedly	create	guess
dream	possible	might

Read Like a Writer, Write for a Reader

A **narrator** is the person who tells the story. A **third-person text** has a narrator that is not a character in the story. A third-person text does not use the words **I** and **me.**

> **The ant** woke early each summer morning. He was a hard worker.

These words show that the narrator is not a character in the story. The narrator tells about the ant.

TURN and TALK Talk to your partner about what you feel when you think about the third-person text *The Ant and the Grasshopper.*

MY TURN Write a third-person sentence about a girl named Sadie. Read your sentence to a partner.

_____

_____

_____

_____

_____

Spell Words with Digraphs and Trigraphs

Digraphs are two letters that spell one sound.
Trigraphs are three letters that spell one sound.

 Sort and spell the words.

Spelling Words			
whale	catch	graph	inch
chin	which	match	check

Digraph

whale

Trigraph

My Words to Know

good   said

Singular and Plural Nouns

A **singular noun** names one noun, as in ant.
A **plural noun** names more than one noun,
as in ants.

Be sure that when you name one thing, you
use a singular noun. When you name more
than one, use a plural noun.

The **plant** is huge. (one plant)
The **boys** are helpful. (more than one boy)

MY TURN Edit the singular and plural
nouns in these sentences.

1. Len ate one plums.

_____
- -
_____

2. We saw three ant.

_____
- -
_____

I can write poetry.

My Learning Goal

Poetry

Poetry can have

- rhyme, rhythm, repetition, alliteration
- words that appeal to the five senses

Race the Rain

Wind in the branches

Repetition — Drip drip on my face

The storm clouds and I

Are in a great race. **Rhyme**

[Splash, splotch, splatter] **Alliteration**

As quick as a flash

I slam the door shut

Just before the first CRASH!

Generate Ideas

Authors think of many ideas before they start drafting, or writing, poetry.

MY TURN What can you write a poem about? Draw pictures to brainstorm your ideas.

Plan Your Poetry

 **MY TURN** Plan your poem. Develop details for one of your ideas from brainstorming.

Poem idea	
Rhyming words	
Repetition	
Alliteration	

What Is a Tricky Character?

Tricky characters often fool other characters. They are clever, or smart.

Tricky characters

- pretend to be honest.
- make others go to the wrong place.
- do not follow rules.
- get others to give them things.

How do tricky characters use their imaginations?

MY TURN Draw your own tricky animal character.

TURN and TALK Tell your partner what your tricky character can do.

Remove Sounds

 **SEE and SAY** Sometimes a sound can be removed, or taken away, to make a new word. Say each picture name. Remove the first sound. Say the new word.

Long o Spelled VCe

The letter **o** makes the long **o** sound you hear in **joke**.

MY TURN Read these words.

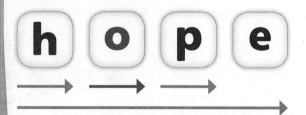

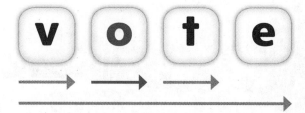

Long o Spelled VCe

TURN and TALK Read these words with a partner.

poke	joke	woke
hope	rope	slope
pole	role	stole
tone	stone	phone

MY TURN Write the letters **o** and **e** to finish the words.

Mike and Kate dig a ____h__l____.

They see part of a ____s_t_n____.

TURN and TALK Now read the sentences.

Read
Together

Long o Spelled VCe

MY TURN Write the word that names each picture.

_____

nose

_____

Remember that long **o** can be spelled **o_e**.

_____

_____

MY TURN Write a sentence about one of the pictures.

_____

_____

_____

Middle Sounds

SEE and SAY Say each picture name. Then say each sound in the picture name.

Long u and Long e Spelled VCe

The letter **u** makes the long **u** sound in **June**.
The letter **e** makes the long **e** sound in **Pete**.

MY TURN Read these words.

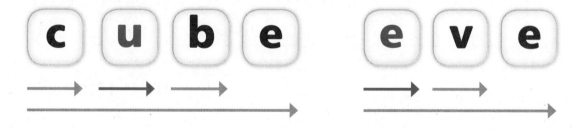

My Words to Know

Some words you must remember and practice.

MY TURN Read these words.

| be | of | old | why | could |

MY TURN Use words from the box to complete the sentences. Then read the sentences.

1. Lots ___of___ kids run by me.

2. They run on the _____ path.

3. _____ do they run?

4. They _____ _____ in a race.

Long u and Long e Spelled VCe

TURN and TALK Read these words with a partner.

| cute | huge | mute |

| theme | Steve | these |

MY TURN Read the sentences.
Underline words with long **u**.
Highlight words with long **e**.

June and Pete have a mule.

The huge mule is cute.

Pete and the mule hum a tune.

June will use a tube.

Zeke will clap for them.

Long u and Long e Spelled VCe

MY TURN Use the words in the box to complete the sentences.

huge	cute	these

1. June has a _cute_ little pet.

2. The pet can catch a _____ ball.

3. Look at _____ paws!

MY TURN Write a sentence about June and her pet.

June _____

_____

_____

The Race

Steve and Pete race home.

Steve the fox is fast.

Pete the cute mule isn't fast.

Could Pete win the race?

Read the story. Highlight the two words that have long **u** spelled VCe.

 AUDIO

Audio with Highlighting

 ANNOTATE

Steve runs past Pete.

Pete looks at his old map.

He chose the close path.

Where could Steve be?

Highlight the four words that have long **e** spelled VCe.

He naps by a wall of <u>stone</u>.

Why did Steve nap?

He ran too fast!

Pete wins the race home!

<u>Underline</u> the two words that have long **o** spelled VCe.

My Learning Goal

I can read traditional stories.

SPOTLIGHT ON GENRE

Folktale

A folktale is a type of traditional story. It is an old story that has been told over and over. It often has a tricky character.

The Tricky Wolf

Long ago, a girl goes to visit her grandma. On the way, she meets a wolf!

Tricky Character

The wolf wants to catch the girl, so he pretends to be her grandma. But the girl runs away!

TURN and TALK Talk about the characters in the folktale.

Folktale Anchor Chart

 short story

 known by many people

 has a simple problem

 can have a tricky character

 has a moral, or lesson, that readers can relate to

The Clever Monkey

Preview Vocabulary

You will read these words in *The Clever Monkey.*

sadly	fairly	exactly	carefully

Read

Look at the structure of the text. It can help you make a prediction. Now make a prediction.

Read to see if the text matches your prediction.

Ask questions about confusing parts.

Talk about what you learned from the text.

Meet the Author

Rob Cleveland is an author, storyteller, actor, and comedian. He has written several children's books and teaches the importance of storytelling to people of all ages.

The Clever Monkey
A folktale from West Africa
as told by Rob Cleveland ◆ illustrated by Baird Hoffmire

In a jungle in West Africa, two cats found a large piece of cheese.

Now these cats loved cheese more than anything.

They could not believe their good fortune.

"How should we divide our cheese?" asked one cat.

"I will be happy to cut it into two equal pieces," said the other cat.

CLOSE READ

<u>Underline</u> the words that help you know the author's purpose.

"How do I know that you will divide it fairly?" asked the first cat. "I will divide the cheese."

"How do I know that you will divide it fairly?" asked the second cat. "I will divide the cheese."

CLOSE READ

Highlight the details that connect to how people in a society, or group, can solve a problem.

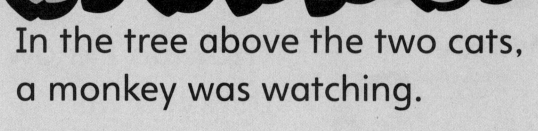

In the tree above the two cats,
a monkey was watching.

Now this monkey also loved cheese
more than just about anything.

He swung down from the tree and went over to the cats.

"I will be happy to divide the cheese into two equal parts for you," said the monkey.

The cats agreed, and after much thought, the monkey divided the cheese into two parts.

The two cats thanked the
monkey and got ready
to eat their cheese.

"Uh-oh," said the monkey.

"I have made a mistake.
The pieces are not equal."

The monkey picked up one of the pieces of cheese.

"Don't worry, I can make them the same size."

VOCABULARY IN CONTEXT

<u>Underline</u> the word that helps you figure out what **equal** means.

The monkey then ate a little bit of the cheese.

"There, now they are the same size."

The cats again thanked the monkey and prepared to enjoy their cheese.

"Uh-oh," said the monkey. "I am afraid that I ate too much. The two pieces are not the same size. But I can fix it."

The monkey then ate a little bit of the other piece of cheese.

"Now," said the monkey, "they are the same size."

CLOSE READ

Underline the details that help you know that the author's purpose is to entertain.

The cats again thanked the
monkey and prepared to enjoy
their cheese.

"Uh-oh," said the monkey. "I did it again. I ate too much. Now the pieces are not the same size, but I can fix it."

CLOSE READ

Highlight the details that help you understand how people in society should treat each other.

"That is alright," said the first cat. "They don't have to be exactly the same size."

"Yes, they do," said the second cat. "We need to have the cheese divided equally."

So the monkey continued trying to divide the cheese into two equal pieces.

The two pieces of cheese became smaller and smaller.

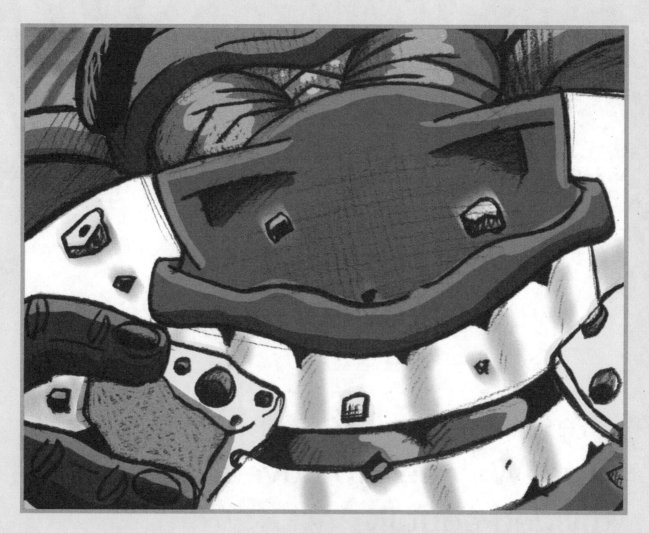

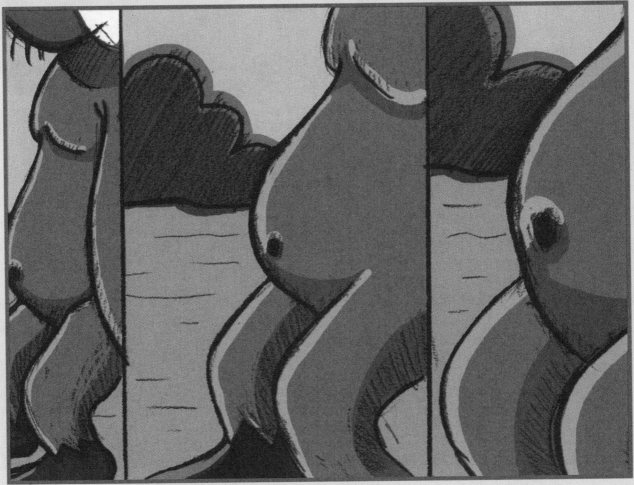

And the monkey's belly got bigger and bigger.

CLOSE READ

<u>Underline</u> the details about the monkey that help you know that the author's purpose is to entertain.

Finally there were two tiny pieces of cheese left. The monkey held them up and looked at them carefully. "I think that these two pieces are exactly the same size. Enjoy your cheese, my friends."

The monkey swung back up into the tree and left the two cats to look sadly at their two tiny pieces of cheese.

CLOSE READ

Highlight how the cats feel when they look at their pieces of cheese. How should people in a society feel when others help them?

"Your piece is bigger,"
said the first cat.

"No, your piece is bigger,"
said the second cat.

"Is not." "Is too." "Is not." "Is too."

For all we know, they are still there arguing, and the clever monkey is still smiling.

CLOSE READ

Highlight what the cats do after they get the cheese from the monkey. After a problem is solved, what should people in a society do?

Develop Vocabulary

The word part **-ly** means **"in a ___ way."**
Happily means **"in a happy way."**

MY TURN Write the meaning of each word.
Use the word part **-ly** to help you.

sadly	in a ꞏꞏsadꞏꞏ way
fairly	in a _____ way
exactly	in an _____ way
carefully	in a _____ way

TURN and TALK Use each word in a sentence
to tell about the text.

Check for Understanding

MY TURN Write the answers to the questions. You can look back at the text.

1. What makes *The Clever Monkey* a folktale?

_____

_____

_____

2. Why do you think the author uses animal characters?

_____

_____

_____

3. What could the cats have done to keep all the cheese? Use text evidence.

_____

_____

_____

Discuss Author's Purpose

Author's purpose is the reason the author writes a text. The purpose can be to inform, to entertain, or to persuade.

MY TURN Underline the author's purpose for writing *The Clever Monkey*. Look back at the text.

> to inform readers about monkeys and cats
>
> to entertain readers about a clever monkey
>
> to persuade readers to eat cheese

How do you know that is the author's purpose?

_____

- -

_____

_____

- -

_____

TURN and TALK Talk about the author's purpose with a partner.

Make Connections

When something you read makes you think of something else, you are making connections. Readers can make connections to the world around them.

MY TURN Write and draw about a lesson everyone can learn from *The Clever Monkey*. Look back at the text.

_____

- -

_____

- -

_____

Reflect and Share

Talk About It

Work with a partner to retell *The Clever Monkey*. What other tricky characters have you read about? How are they like the clever monkey?

Share Information and Ideas

When talking with others, it is important to:

- Ask questions when you do not understand something.

- Answer questions in complete sentences.

Use the words on the note to help you.

Now share your ideas.

> What do you mean when you say . . . ?

Weekly Question

How do tricky characters use their imaginations?

Read Together

I can make and use words to connect reading and writing.

Academic Vocabulary

Synonyms are words that have similar meanings.
Antonyms are words that have opposite meanings.

MY TURN Read the words in each row.
Write **S** on the line if the words are synonyms.
Write **A** on the line if the words are antonyms.

suppose	pretend	S
possible	impossible	
create	destroy	
imagine	invent	

Read Like a Writer, Write for a Reader

Authors choose words to help describe details in a text.

The two **pieces of cheese** became smaller and smaller. ◀····· And the **monkey's belly** got bigger and bigger.

The author chose these words to help describe the cheese and the monkey's belly.

MY TURN Write sentences that tell about something the monkey does. The words should describe the action.

_____

- -

_____

- -

_____

- -

_____

- -

_____

Read Together

Spell Long o Words

Long **o** words can be spelled **o_e**.

MY TURN Sort and spell the words. Then find five words in a dictionary.

-one

bone

_____

_____

-ope

_____

_____

_____

-ose

_____

_____

_____

-oke

_____

_____

_____

My Words to Know

_____

_____

_____

Spelling Words

joke

rope

hope

stone

rose

bone

broke

those

My Words to Know

why

could

Common and Proper Nouns

A **common noun** names any person, place, or thing.

A **proper noun** names a special or particular person, place, or thing.

Be sure to capitalize proper nouns.

The **park** is on the busy **street.** (common nouns)
Central Park is on **Main Street.** (proper nouns)

MY TURN Edit the common and proper nouns in these sentences.

1. My Dog is big.

_____

2. Her name is molly.

_____

3. We walked to pike park.

_____

My Learning Goal

I can write poetry.

The Five Senses

Authors use words to describe how things look, smell, sound, feel, and taste.

MY TURN Write a word or phrase for each sense that you can use in your poem.

Sight	
Sound	
Smell	
Touch	
Taste	

POETRY

Compose Imagery

Imagery is the way authors use words to create pictures in readers' minds. The words make readers use their five senses.

The bright yellow sunflower blooms.

MY TURN Look for examples of imagery in poems you have read. Write the words that make you create pictures in your mind.

_____
_____
_____
_____
_____
_____

MY TURN Write words and phrases for your poem that will create pictures in the readers' minds.

Word Choice

Authors choose words carefully. They choose words they think will be interesting and exciting for readers.

MY TURN Write some words and phrases you read in poems that you thought were interesting.

_____

- -

_____

- -

_____

- -

_____

- -

_____

MY TURN Add interesting words and phrases as you write your poem.

New Ideas!

author

The
Blackout
written by Zetta Elliott illustrated by
Maxime Lebrun

Zetta Elliott wrote this story. She used her imagination to create the characters, setting, and events.

Alexander Graham Bell invented the telephone a long time ago. The telephone looks very different today.

inventor

How can imagination lead to a new idea?

Ellen Ochoa
had new ideas about
how to get better
pictures of space.

astronaut

TURN and **TALK** Which new idea do you like best? How did imagination help these people think of new ideas?

 Read Together

Remove Sounds

 **SEE and SAY** Sometimes a sound can be removed, or taken away, to make a new word. Say each picture name. Then remove, or take away, the last sound in each picture name. Say the new words.

Long e Spelled e, ee

Long **e** can be spelled **e** as in **me**.
Long **e** can be spelled **ee** as in **bee**.

MY TURN Read these words.

Long e Spelled e, ee

TURN and TALK Read these words with a partner.

be	me	we
he	she	see
feel	week	sweep
keep	meet	green

MY TURN Write **e** or **ee** to finish each word. Read the sentences.

1. Look at the bug with ___m___!

2. The ___b___ can buzz.

Long e Spelled e, ee

MY TURN Say each picture name. Write the long **e** word that names the picture.

Long **e** is spelled **ee** in these picture names.

bee

_____

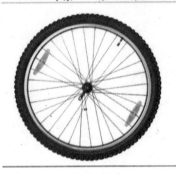

MY TURN Write a sentence about one of the long **e** picture names.

_____

_____

_____

_____

Segment and Blend Sounds

 **SEE and SAY** Say each picture name. Then segment the sounds in the picture name. Blend the sounds to say the picture name again.

  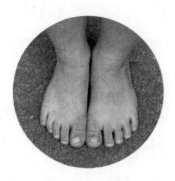

Inflectional Ending -ed

Sometimes a word is made up of a base word or root and an ending. The **-ed** ending on a verb shows that the action happened in the past.

 **MY TURN** Write **ed** at the end of each word. Read the words.

jump   help

 **TURN and TALK** Use each word in a sentence.

My Words to Know

Some words you must remember and practice.

MY TURN Read these words.

or	out	who	live	work

MY TURN Complete the poem with words from the box.

Handwriting Print the words legibly, or clearly.

Who ____ are you?

Do you like to run _____ and in?

Do you like to yell _____ grin?

Do you _____ in a home by me?

Do you like to _____ with Lee?

Inflectional Ending -ed

TURN and TALK Decode these words with a partner. Use the ending to tell what each word means.

helped	**wished**	**fixed**
missed	**needed**	**yelled**
peeled	**tested**	**hunted**
kicked	**planted**	**greeted**

MY TURN Write **ed** to finish each word. Read the sentences.

1. Dee ___lift___ the bag of sand.

2. She ___ask___ me for help.

Inflectional Ending -ed

MY TURN Read the words. Use the words in the box to complete the sentences.

filled	buzzed	rented

1. We __rented__ a home by a hive.

2. The bees _____.

3. They _____ the hive.

MY TURN Write a sentence that includes a base word or root with the ending **-ed**.

_____

_____

_____

_____

A Deep Sleep

Dee came home from work late.

Who can help Dee sleep?

The sheep live out by Dee.

They feel like they need to help.

Read the story. Highlight the nine words with the long **e** sound.

AUDIO
Audio with Highlighting

ANNOTATE

115

They walked up to Dee.

"You came to see me?"
she asked.

"We can help you sleep,"
they said.

Underline the three words with the
long **e** sound spelled **e**.

Dee went back to bed.

The sheep tell her a sweet tale.

She rested on her cheek.

Dee drifted into a deep sleep.

Highlight the two words with an inflectional ending.

My Learning Goal

I can read about using my imagination.

Poetry

A poem has words written in lines. Some poems have repetition, or when words repeat. Some poems have alliteration, or when words begin with the same sound.

Silly Animal Sights

Alliteration → A chick that cheers

A horse in a hat

A dog that dances . . .

Repetition → Imagine that, imagine that!

TURN and TALK Talk about how a poem, a fable, and a folktale are alike and different.

Poetry Anchor Chart

Rhyme

The pup fit in the cup.
Let's pick it up!

Rhythm

Jack and Jill went up
a hill to fetch a pail
of water

Repetition

Row, row, row
your boat

Alliteration

For days and days,
the dancer dances

Poetry Collection

Preview Vocabulary

You will read these words in the poems this week.

draw	doodle	decorate	scribble

Read

Read the titles and make a prediction. Then read the poems.

Look at the pictures to help you understand what the poems are about.

Ask questions to clarify information.

Talk about whether your predictions were right.

Meet the Author

Sharon Wooding is the author of "The Box." She has written many books and poems for children. Sometimes she creates the pictures, too.

Poetry Collection

Poodle Doodles *by Jean Hansen-Novak*

The Box *by Sharon Wooding*

Sandcastle *by Carol A. Grund*

AUDIO

Audio with Highlighting

ANNOTATE

Poodle Doodles

by Jean Hansen-Novak
illustrated by Matt Smith

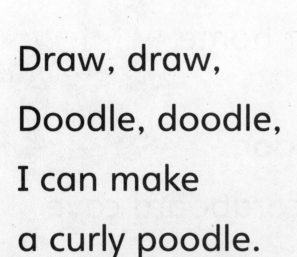

Draw, draw,

Doodle, doodle,

I can make

a curly poodle.

Draw, draw,

Scribble, scribble.

Now I'll make

A bone to nibble!

CLOSE READ

<u>Underline</u> the words in the poem
that repeat.

The Box

by Sharon Wooding
illustrated by Lynne Cravath

When Dad brought home
the great big box
And left it by my door,
I crawled inside a cardboard cave
And roared a dragon's roar.

Then one day Daddy carved a little
Hole into the box.
The cave became a fox's den,
And I became a fox.

Still later I drew flowers on

The cardboard, and a tree.

Dad cut some doors and
windows out,

And now I'm being me.

CLOSE READ

Underline the three word pairs that begin with the same sound.

Sandcastle

by Carol A. Grund
illustrated by John Sandford

Soft and squishy, wet and
brown—

Scoop the sand and pack it down.

Fill a bucket, fill a cup,

Dump it out, then build it up.

Here a tower, there a wall,

Now a moat surrounds it all.

Gather sticks to make a gate,

Shells and stones to decorate.

Waves reach up and lick the
shore,

Knocking at our castle door.

Soon it all will melt away . . .

Come and build another day!

CLOSE READ

Highlight ideas in this poem that you can connect to ideas in the other poems.

127

Develop Vocabulary

MY TURN Follow the directions to create a picture using your imagination.

Draw a picture of yourself.

Doodle something around the picture.

Scribble lines by the picture.

Decorate your picture.

Check for Understanding

MY TURN Write the answers to the questions. You can look back at the texts.

1. How can you tell these texts are poems?

_____
_____
_____
_____

2. Why does the author of "Sandcastle" use rhyming words?

_____
_____
_____
_____

3. Why does a sandcastle melt away? Use text evidence.

_____
_____
_____
_____

Find Elements of Poetry

Repetition is when words or phrases repeat.
Alliteration is when words begin
with the same sound.

MY TURN Circle the example of each poem
element. Look back at the text.

Repetition

Now I'll make A bone to nibble!	Draw, draw Doodle, doodle

Alliteration

big box cardboard cave	dragon's roar fox's den

TURN and TALK Why do you think authors use
repetition and alliteration in poems?

Make Connections

When something you read makes you think of something else, you are making connections. One way to make connections is to figure out how two or more texts are similar and different.

MY TURN Draw and write what the three poems are about. Look back at the text.

The poems are about _____

Reflect and Share

Talk About It

You read three poems about using imagination. In your own words, tell which poem you like the best and why you like it best. Use examples from the poems to explain why.

Sharing Your Opinion

When sharing your opinion, it is important to:

- Say your opinion clearly.

- Give a reason to support your opinion.

Use the words on the note to help you.

I think ___ because ___.

Now share your opinion in a complete sentence.

Weekly Question

How can imagination lead to a new idea?

I can make and use words to connect reading and writing.

My Learning Goal

Academic Vocabulary

Context clues are words or pictures that can help you figure out what unknown words mean.

MY TURN Read each sentence. Highlight the context clues for the underlined word.

1. She had many <u>possibilities</u> and choices to doodle.

2. I use my <u>imagination</u> to think of new ideas.

3. I'm not sure, but I <u>suppose</u> we can build a tall sandcastle.

Read Like a Writer, Write for a Reader

Authors often use rhyming words in poems. Rhyming words have the same middle and ending sounds.

Gather sticks to make
a gate, Shells and stones ◄········
to decorate.

The author uses rhyming words to make the poem fun to read.

MY TURN Write two or more sentences with rhyming words. Your sentences can be silly!

Spell Long e Words

The end of these open syllable words is spelled **e** or **ee**.

 **MY TURN** Sort and spell the words.

Spelling Words

see	me	tree	we
she	be	he	three

e

me

ee

My Words to Know

live	work

Pronouns

A **pronoun** takes the place of a noun.

She likes to doodle. (subjective pronoun)
It is **their** box. (possessive pronoun)
Can you give it to **me?** (objective pronoun)
We play with **everyone!** (indefinite pronoun)

MY TURN Edit the sentences by replacing the underlined word or words with a pronoun.

1. <u>Dad</u> is here.

   He _____ is here.

2. We play with the box <u>that belongs to Dad</u>.

   _____

   We play with _____ box.

3. Do you know <u>the girl</u>?

   _____

   Do you know _____?

My Learning Goal

I can write poetry.

Line Breaks and White Space

A **line break** is where the author chooses to end one line and begin a new line.
White space is the area around a poem.

 **MY TURN** (Circle) the word before each line break. Draw a picture in the white space.

Draw, (draw),

Scribble, scribble.

Now I'll make

A bone to nibble!

MY TURN Include line breaks and white space as you write your poem.

137

Sound Words

Sound words are words that represent a sound. **Click** and **bam** are sound words.

MY TURN Look at each picture. Write a sound word that describes the picture.

_____
- -
_____

_____
- -
_____

_____
- -
_____

_____
- -
_____

MY TURN Include sound words as you write your poem.

Rhyme

Rhyming words have the same middle and ending sounds. Authors often use rhyming words to make poetry fun to read.

MY TURN Read the poem. Highlight the rhyming words.

> Drip, drop!
>
> Will it stop?
>
> Flip, flop!
>
> We need a mop.

MY TURN Write a line that rhymes with the poem.

_____

_____

_____

MY TURN Write your poem using rhyme.

Stories Tell About . . .

A place we haven't traveled before,

all of the people who live shore to shore,

an event from the past that might affect me,

How can stories help us learn lessons?

and what we suppose
the future could be.

MY TURN Think about a story you have read.
Draw something new you learned from the story.

Final Sounds

 SEE and SAY Say each picture name. Listen to the final sound as you name each picture. Then say each picture name again.

Vowel Sounds of y

Long **i** can be spelled **y**, as in **my**.

Long **e** can be spelled **y**, as in **body**.

 Read each word.

w h y   c i t y

Vowel Sounds of y

TURN and TALK Read these words. Name the vowel sound y makes in each word.

my	by	shy
sleepy	windy	copy
try	dry	fry
happy	funny	silly

MY TURN Say each picture name. Write y to finish each word. Then read the words.

cr_____

cit_____

Vowel Sounds of y

 **MY TURN** Write **y** to finish the words. Then read the sentences.

1. Look up at the ___sk**y**___ .

2. The hawks ___fl___ .

3. They are ___speed___ hawks.

First, try long **i** for the sound of **y**. Then try long **e**.

 **MY TURN** Write another sentence that includes a word with the vowel sound spelled **y**.

_____

- -

_____

- -

_____

Segment and Blend Sounds

SEE and SAY To make words, we segment, or separate, sounds and then blend, or combine, them. Segment the sounds in each picture name. Then blend them.

Syllable Pattern VCCV

A **syllable** is a word part with a vowel sound. A **closed syllable** is closed off by a consonant. A word with two consonants in the middle is divided between the consonants.

MY TURN Read the word. Draw a line to show where to divide the word into syllables.

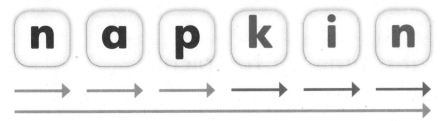

Read Together

My Words to Know

Some words you must remember and practice.

MY TURN Read these words.

now	down	there	drink	together

MY TURN Write words from the box to complete the sentences. Read the sentences.

1. We can have a picnic together.

2. Get a _____ from _____.

3. We need to sit _____.

4. _____ it is time for the picnic!

Syllable Pattern VCCV

TURN and TALK Read these words.

dentist	picnic	fabric
indent	plastic	rabbit
reptile	until	basket
tennis	mitten	public

MY TURN Say each picture name. Write the two-syllable words. Read the words.

_____   _____

Syllable Pattern VCCV

MY TURN Read the sentences. <u>Underline</u> the two-syllable words.

<u>Matty</u> is happy to see Patty.

They are in a tennis match.

The match happens in the summer.

"Good luck!" Matty says to Patty.

MY TURN Write a new sentence about Matty and Patty.

Matty and Patty

The Picnic

Bandit the kitten has a picnic.

He asks Lily the rabbit to come.

Bandit gets a basket.

He takes napkins and a drink.

AUDIO

Audio with Highlighting

ANNOTATE

Read the story. Highlight the two-syllable words that divide into closed syllables.

Bandit comes to the <u>city</u>.

Lily is not there.

He sits down and gets weepy.

Lily comes by too late.

<u>Underline</u> the four words with the long **e** sound spelled **y**.

Now she sees Bandit cry.

She feels bad.

Lily sits by him and smiles.

Together they have fun!

Highlight the two words with the long **i** sound spelled **y**.

My Learning Goal I can read traditional stories.

SPOTLIGHT ON GENRE

Fable

A fable sometimes has animal characters that talk and act like people.

TURN and TALK How do these characters act like people?

Be a Fluent Reader Fluent readers read at an appropriate rate. That means they do not read too fast or too slow. After you read this week's text, practice reading fluently with a partner.

Fable Anchor Chart

Describe Characters

- what they do
- what they say
- how they feel
- the reasons for their actions

The Cow and the Tiger

Preview Vocabulary

You will read these words in *The Cow and the Tiger*.

sad	angry	happy	surprised

Read

Read to find the most important ideas.

Look for details to help you describe and visualize the setting and events.

Ask questions during reading to understand the text.

Talk about the moral of the text.

Meet the Author

Sudha Ramaswami teaches second grade. She has written two children's books that teach the importance of doing the right thing. She loves to write poetry too.

AUDIO

Audio with Highlighting

ANNOTATE

THE COW AND THE TIGER

written by
Sudha Ramaswami

illustrated by
Kasia Nowowiejska

Once there was a cow named Bala. She had a beautiful calf. Bala liked to graze in the shadowy forest and then feed her calf.

One day, Bala went to the forest. An angry tiger caught her. Sad Bala cried, "Please don't eat me! Let me go feed my calf."

CLOSE READ

What can you visualize about the forest? Highlight the details that help you.

Bala said, "I promise, I promise to come back.

I'll come back soon. Then you can attack!"

Tiger agreed. Bala went back to her grassy home. She quickly fed her calf. Then she returned to the shadowy forest and looked for Tiger.

CLOSE READ

<u>Underline</u> the words that describe where Bala lives.

Bala said, "I promised, I promised that I'd come back."

Tiger was surprised to see her. He was pleased that Bala kept her word.

Tiger said, "You promised, you promised that you'd come back. You told the truth. Now I won't attack."

CLOSE READ

<u>Underline</u> why Tiger does not attack Bala.

Bala was very happy. She went back to her calf.

Tiger was not mad anymore. He promised, he promised to protect Bala from other animals.

Moral: Always keep your promises. Always tell the truth.

FLUENCY

Read pages 160–161 aloud with a partner to practice reading at an appropriate rate.

Develop Vocabulary

 MY TURN Read the clues. Then use the words in the box to complete the crossword puzzle.

sad	angry	happy	surprised

2 **3**

1 s u r p r i s e d

Across	Down
1.	1.
2.	3.

Check for Understanding

MY TURN Write the answer to each question. You can look back at the text.

1. What makes this text a fable?

_____

_____

_____

_____

2. Why does the author use the word **cried?**

_____

_____

_____

_____

3. How do the characters' actions show the moral, or lesson? Use text evidence.

_____

_____

_____

_____

Describe Main Events and Setting

Main events are the important events in a story. The **setting** is when and where a story happens.

MY TURN Describe the main event when Bala comes back. Look back at the text.

_____

- -

_____

- -

_____

- -

_____

MY TURN Draw a picture of Bala's home. Look back at the text.

Visualize Details

The details in a story help readers make pictures in their minds about the setting and events.

MY TURN Draw how you see the forest. Look back at the text.

The Forest

Reflect and Share

Write to Sources

You read a fable with a moral. What is another fable you read? How are the fables alike and different? On a separate sheet of paper, write comments that compare and contrast the fables.

Use Text Evidence

When writing comments on two texts, it is important to:

- Find examples from both texts that support your ideas.

- Explain how the text evidence supports your ideas.

Weekly Question

How can stories help us learn lessons?

I can make and use words to connect reading and writing.

My Learning Goal

Academic Vocabulary

Word parts can be added to some words to make new words with new meanings.

The word part **-less** means "**without.**"
The word part **-ful** means "**full of.**"

MY TURN Match the words to their meanings.

hopeful   full of thought

shapeless   full of hope

thoughtful   without shape

Read Like a Writer, Write for a Reader

Authors use words to help readers visualize how characters feel as they speak.

Sad Bala cried, "Please don't eat me!"

The author chose this word to help readers picture how Bala feels as she talks.

TURN and TALK Talk with a partner about what you visualize when you read the word **cried.**

MY TURN Write some words that describe how a character can say something. The words should help you picture how the character feels.

_____

- - - - - - - - - - - - - - - - - -

_____

- - - - - - - - - - - - - - - - - -

_____

- - - - - - - - - - - - - - - - - -

_____

- - - - - - - - - - - - - - - - - -

Read Together

Spell Words with the Vowel Sounds of y

Long **i** and long **e** can be spelled **y** at the end of a word. **Alphabetize** means to put a series, or list, of words in order of the alphabet. Look at the first letters. If the first letters are the same, look at the second letters.

MY TURN Alphabetize the words.

1. by

2. _____

3. _____

4. _____

5. _____

6. _____

7. _____

8. _____

9. _____

10. _____

Spelling Words
my
silly
try
fly
why
cry
by
puppy

My Words to Know

there

now

Read Together

Pronouns I and me

Pronouns are words that take the place of nouns. The pronouns **I** and **me** take the place of your own name. Use a capital letter to write **I**. Always name yourself last.

Kate and **I** left. (subject pronoun)
Kate is with **me**. (object pronoun)

MY TURN Edit the pronouns **I** and **me** in these sentences. Cross out the wrong pronoun. Write the correct pronoun.

1. You and ~~me~~ go to school. _____ I _____

2. Should i take the bus? _____

3. Meet I inside. _____

I can write poetry.

Edit for Pronouns

A **pronoun** takes the place of a noun.
Subjective: I, you, he, she, it, we, they
Objective: me, you, him, her, it, us, them
Possessive: my, your, his, her, its, our, their

MY TURN Write the pronoun that can replace the underlined words.

1. <u>The doll</u> broke. _I_

2. It is <u>Bea's</u> doll. _____

3. Give the doll to <u>Jan and Ken.</u> _____

MY TURN Edit for pronouns in your poem.

Edit for Spelling

Authors edit, or fix, their spelling. They can use spelling patterns and rules to check some words. They need to remember how to spell other words.

Let's get **owt** of the **lak**.   out   lake

MY TURN Edit these sentences. Underline the word that is not spelled correctly. Write it correctly.

1. Jen and Ken run in a rase.   race

2. They run togeter. _____

3. Who will win the conntest? _____

4. I thingk Jen will win now. _____

MY TURN Edit for spelling in your poem.

Edit for Adverbs That Convey Time

Authors use adverbs to tell more about verbs and adjectives. Adverbs tell how, when, or where something happens.

She **always** keeps her promises. (tells when)

 **MY TURN** Use an adverb from the box to finish each sentence.

soon	later	always

1. Finish your book later!

   _____

2. We _____ read new books.

   _____

3. Will you be done reading _____?

MY TURN Edit your poem for adverbs.

Creative Expression

Types of Music

Classical

Musicians in an orchestra often play classical music together.

flute

violin

cello

trumpet

Blues

Blues singers tell how they feel in their music.

guitar

harmonica

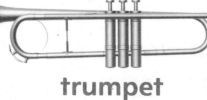

Why are art and music classes important?

Forms of Art

Painting

Impressionist paintings show nature and people with soft colors and a lot of light.

Pottery

Objects are made from clay and then dried with heat.

TURN and TALK Talk with a partner about art and music you want to learn more about.

Final Sounds

 **SEE and SAY** Say each sound as you name each picture. Tell the final sound you hear in each picture name.

Consonant Patterns ng, nk

The letters **ng** make the sound at the end of **ring**.
The letters **nk** make the sound at the end of **sink**.

MY TURN Read these words.

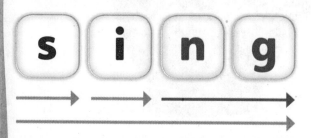

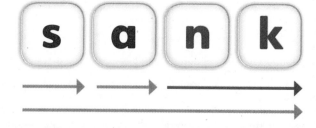

Consonant Patterns ng, nk

TURN and TALK Read these words.

bank	**tank**	**sank**
blink	**drink**	**think**
bang	**hang**	**rang**
sing	**ring**	**sting**

MY TURN Say each picture name.
Circle the letters that spell the final sound.

nk   ng

nk   ng

Consonant Patterns ng, nk

MY TURN Write **ng** or **nk** to finish the words. Then read the sentences.

"Look at this __junk__!" said Ling.

"__Bri____ me a box," she said.

"I __thi____ it will all fit."

MY TURN Write what Ling says next. Use a word with **ng** or **nk**.

_____

_____

_____

Syllables

 **SEE and SAY** Say each picture name. Then break each word into syllables, or word parts, and say each syllable.

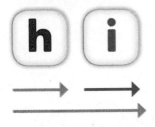  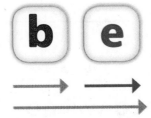

Open Syllables

A **syllable** is a word part with a vowel sound. An **open syllable** ends in a vowel. It usually has a long vowel sound. When a word or syllable has only one consonant and one vowel, the vowel sound is usually long.

 **MY TURN** Read these words.

| h | i | | g | o | | b | e |

My Words to Know

Some words you must remember and practice.

MY TURN Read these words.

| grow | full | find | under | around |

MY TURN Complete each sentence with a word from the box. Read the sentences.

1. The bag is _full_ of seeds.

2. The kids glance _____ .

3. They will _____ plants here.

4. They _____ a spot to dig.

5. A seed will go _____ there.

Open Syllables

TURN and TALK Decode these words with open syllables.

so	**we**	**no**
me	**be**	**he**
lilac	**banjo**	**pilot**
motor	**tiny**	**hotel**

MY TURN Write **o**, **e**, or **i** to finish the words.

1. Hi Mo! Can W go?

2. N! Do not g!

TURN and TALK Now read the sentences.

Open Syllables

MY TURN Read the sentences. <u>Underline</u> words with an open syllable.

The <u>ro</u>bot said hello to me.

He had a tiny banjo.

It had to be reset.

We could go donate it.

An open syllable has a long vowel sound.

MY TURN Write a sentence about a robot. Use a word with an open syllable.

_____

- -

_____

- -

_____

- -

_____

Sing!

Link and Tony go to class.

The class is full of kids.

Miss King asks the class to sing.

They blink and grow silent.

Read the story. Highlight the three words with an open syllable.

 AUDIO

Audio with Highlighting

 ANNOTATE

Link and Tony glance around.

Link gets up to <u>sing</u> a solo.

Tony can bring a bell to ring.

They find a spot under the pink kite.

<u>Underline</u> the three words that end with **ng**.

Miss King <u>winks</u> at Link and Tony.

Link grabs a banjo.

Link and Tony think singing is fun!

<u>Underline</u> the five words that end with **nk.**

My Learning Goal

I can read about using my imagination.

Persuasive Text

A persuasive text tries to get readers to think or act in a certain way. The author gives an opinion and reasons. The author uses persuasive words, such as **should** or **must**.

Soccer Is Great

Opinion — Soccer is the best sport.

Reasons — You can play anywhere because all you need is a ball. Soccer is great exercise. It's fun to be part of a team.

TURN and TALK How is persuasive text different from a traditional story?

Persuasive Text Anchor Chart

Opinion

what the author tries to persuade the reader to think or do.

Reasons

why the author thinks or believes something

Thumbs Up for Art and Music!

Preview Vocabulary

You will read these words in *Thumbs Up for Art and Music!*

learn	think	remember	concentrate

Read

Read to understand what the author wants you to think or do.

Look for reasons the author gives.

Ask questions to clarify information.

Talk about your personal connection to this text.

Meet the Author

Greg Leitich Smith writes adventure stories. His books feature a lot of humor, science, art, and music.

Thumbs Up for Art and Music!

written by Greg Leitich Smith

 AUDIO

Audio with Highlighting

 ANNOTATE

191

In school you learn to read and write. You learn to do math problems. Reading, writing, and math are important.

Some people don't think art in school is important, but I do! Here is why.

CLOSE READ

Highlight the words that tell what happens at school.

Art is important because you learn to be creative. You have to use your imagination.

Art is important because it makes you think. You figure out how to make amazing things.

CLOSE READ

Underline what the author wants readers to think and why the author thinks that.

Some people don't think music in school is important, but I do! Here is why.

Music is important because it makes you concentrate. You have to remember a lot.

CLOSE READ

Underline what the author wants readers to think and why the author thinks that.

Music is important because you can play with others. You learn about teamwork.

There are many reasons having art and music in school is important, but this is the best one. They are fun!

CLOSE READ

Underline why the author thinks art and music in school are important.

Develop Vocabulary

MY TURN Write the word from the box that best completes each sentence.

think	learn	remember	concentrate

We learn to be creative in art.

Music needs us to focus or _____.

Art makes us _____ and figure things out.

We must _____ things in music.

TURN and TALK Use the words in your own sentences.

Check for Understanding

MY TURN Write the answers to the questions. You can look back at the text.

1. What makes this text a persuasive text?

_____

_____

_____

_____

2. Why does the author use photos?

_____

_____

_____

_____

3. Do you think it is important to have art and music at school? Use text evidence.

_____

_____

_____

_____

Identify Persuasive Text

Authors of persuasive text try to persuade readers to think or do something. They use reasons to support their opinion.

MY TURN What is the author trying to persuade readers to think in *Thumbs Up for Art and Music!?* Look back at the text.

_____

_____

_____

_____

_____

_____

TURN and TALK Talk with a partner about the reasons the author uses to persuade readers.

Make Connections

Readers make connections when what they read makes them think of something else. Readers can connect what they read to their personal experiences.

MY TURN What does this text make you think about in your life? Draw a connection you can make. Look back at the text.

Reflect and Share

Talk About It

Retell the reasons the author uses to persuade readers in *Thumbs Up for Art and Music!* What do you think about art and music classes?

- -

Retell Texts

When you retell a text, it is important to:

- Tell the information in your own words.

- Include the key ideas and details.

- Maintain, or keep, the same meaning as the text.

- -

Weekly Question

Why are art and music classes important?

I can make and use words to connect reading and writing.

My Learning Goal

Academic Vocabulary

 **MY TURN** Draw a picture for this sentence.

In my imagination, I can create things that are supposed to be impossible!

TURN and TALK Explain how your picture connects to the sentence.

Read Like a Writer, Write for a Reader

In persuasive text, authors use persuasive words and phrases to help convince readers to think or do something.

> You have to use your imagination.

◀······· The author uses this phrase to persuade readers to use their imaginations.

MY TURN Write a sentence with a persuasive word, such as **should**, **must**, or **best**.

_____

- -

_____

- -

_____

- -

_____

- -

_____

Spell Words with Consonant Patterns ng, nk

Sometimes two letters combine to make one sound, as in **ng** in **sang** and **nk** in **sink**.

 **MY TURN** Sort and spell the words.

-ng

ring

-nk

My Words to Know

Spelling Words
ring
bring
pink
sing
song
think
thing
rink

My Words to Know

grow

around

Capitalization

A **proper name** begins with a capital letter. The pronoun **I** is always a capital letter. **Days** and **months** begin with capital letters.

Do you have art class with **Mia?**
Mia and **I** made art.
Music class is on **Tuesday, May** 10.

MY TURN Edit for capital letters in these sentences. Write the words that need a capital letter.

1. The art fair is in june.

June

2. Tim and i will sing with jess.

3. Will i get to play the song on monday?

My Learning Goal

I can write poetry.

Edit for Nouns

A noun names a person, place, or thing.

Singular noun: marker
Plural noun: markers
Common noun: girl
Proper noun: Beth

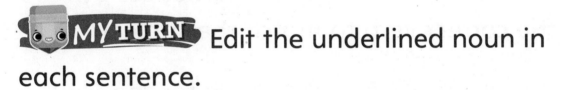 **MY TURN** Edit the underlined noun in each sentence.

1. Grab these <u>pen</u>.

pens

2. Let's draw the <u>Dog</u>.

3. His <u>tails</u> is short.

4. His name is <u>max</u>.

MY TURN Edit the nouns in your poem.

Edit for Complete Sentences with Subject-Verb Agreement

The subject and verb in a sentence must agree. Add **-s** to a verb that tells what one person, animal, or thing is doing now.
Do not add **-s** to verbs that tell what two or more people, animals, and things are doing now.

MY TURN Edit the complete sentences by circling the correct verb to match the subject.

The boys and girls (get / gets) ready for the play.

They (paint / paints) the props.

Sam (make / makes) the costumes.

Jess and Tim (move / moves) the lights.

MY TURN Edit your poem for complete sentences with subject-verb agreement.

Publish and Celebrate

MY TURN Use the checklist to help get your poem ready to publish, or share.

☐ I used words that appeal to the five senses.

☐ I used line breaks and white space.

☐ I used imagery and interesting words.

☐ I edited for subject-verb agreement.

TURN and TALK Share your poem. Express the needs and feelings you had during writing.

UNIT THEME

Imagine That

 **TURN** and **TALK**

Look back at each text. Find a word or phrase from each text that you can connect to the word **imagination**.

Poetry Collection

"Poodle Doodles"
"The Box" "Sandcastle"

WEEK 3

BOOK CLUB

WEEK 2

The Clever Monkey

BOOK CLUB

WEEK 1

The Ant and the Grasshopper

The Cow and
the Tiger

WEEK
4

WEEK
5 Thumbs Up for
Art and Music!

Essential Question

MY TURN

How can we use our
imaginations?

BOOK
CLUB

Project

WEEK
6

Now it's time to apply what
you learned about imaginations
in your **WEEK 6 PROJECT:**
More than a Tale.

Segment and Blend Sounds

 **SEE and SAY** Say each picture name. Then say each sound in the picture name. Blend the sounds to say the picture names again.

r-Controlled Vowels **or**, **ore**

When the letter **r** comes after a vowel, the vowel makes a special sound. The letters **or** and **ore** make the vowel sound in **horn** and **store**.

MY TURN Read the words.

r-Controlled Vowels or, ore

TURN and TALK Decode these words with a partner.

or	**wore**	**shore**
tore	**snore**	**chore**
born	**corn**	**thorn**
fort	**sort**	**sport**

MY TURN Read these sentences. Underline words with **or** or **ore.**

We take a <u>short</u> drive to the <u>shore</u>.

I wore my cap from the store.

We make a sand fort and then swim more!

r-Controlled Vowels or, ore

MY TURN Add **or** or **ore**. Read each word. Then draw a line from each word to its picture.

c	o	r	n
h			n
s	c		
s	t		

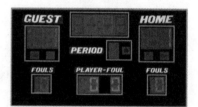

MY TURN Write a sentence about things at a store. Use at least one word with **or** or **ore**.

A store has

Read Together

Spell r-Controlled or, ore Words

The letters **or** and **ore** spell the vowel sound in **horn** and **tore**.

MY TURN Sort and spell the words. Then find four spelling words in a dictionary.

ore

sore

or

My Words to Know

Spelling Words

or

form

torn

sore

more

storm

score

store

My Words to Know

their

some

217

Segment and Blend Sounds

SEE and SAY Say each picture name. Then say the smaller words that make up each word.

Compound Words

A **compound word** is made up of two smaller words joined together. When you see a long word, check to see whether there are two smaller words in it: backpack = back + pack. Read each smaller word, and then read the compound word.

MY TURN Read this compound word.

My Words to Know

Some words you must remember and practice.

MY TURN Read these words.

so	eat	play	their	some

MY TURN Complete each sentence with a word or words from the box. Read the sentences.

1. Lenore and Sam _eat_ hot dogs.

2. Then they have _____ popcorn.

3. They see _____ team _____ baseball.

4. Cheering at the game is _____ much fun!

Compound Words

TURN and TALK Read these words. Name the two smaller words in each compound word.

bathtub	**pancakes**
popcorn	**bedtime**
sidewalk	**sandbox**
homemade	**notepad**
baseball	**treetop**

MY TURN Read the words. Draw a line between the two words that make up each compound word.

weekend   beehive   checkup

Compound Words

MY TURN Draw lines to join words to make three compound words.

back   thing

some   shine

sun   bone

Try **back** with **thing**, **shine**, and **bone** to find the compound word.

MY TURN Write a sentence with one of the compound words you made.

_____

_____

_____

_____

What Now?

 AUDIO

Audio with Highlighting

 ANNOTATE

Lenore and Sam can't play more.

It is time to eat.

So they go back to their home.

They do chores before bedtime.

Read the story. Highlight the four
words with the **or** sound spelled **ore.**

What can Lenore do this weekend?

She goes to play in the sunshine.

No one is there by the hillside.

Underline the three **compound words**.

Sam can't play sports now.

So Lenore looks for her backpack.

She gets some pens and a notepad.

She draws for fun!

Highlight the four words with the **or** sound.

More than a Tale

Activity

Write an opinion text about why we should read folktales. Use examples to support your ideas. Include a picture.

RESEARCH

Let's Read!

This week you will read three articles that will help you write an opinion text.

1 Folktales

2 Dance On!

3 Use Your Imagination

 **COLLABORATE** With a partner, generate two questions for your research about folktales.

Use Academic Words

COLLABORATE You learned many new academic words in this unit. With your partner, talk about the picture. Remember to use these words in your opinion text.

Folktale Research Plan

Day 1 Generate questions for research.

Day 2 Conduct research.

Day 3 Write an opinion text.

Day 4 Revise and edit your text.

Day 5 Present your text to the class.

Why Should I Think That?

Sometimes authors try to persuade you to think or do something. Think about the reasons authors use.

COLLABORATE With a partner, read "Dance On!" Then fill in the chart about the article.

What does the author want you to think?	
What reasons does the author use?	
What persuasive words does the author use?	

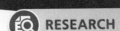
Look and Listen

Video and sound recordings can help you hear and see folktales. Watch or listen closely. Take notes to gather information.

COLLABORATE Write the name of a folktale you will watch or listen to with a partner.

_____

- -

_____

Write two ideas from the recording.

_____

1. _____

_____

2. _____

Persuasive Text

A good writer gives a strong opinion and uses persuasive words to get the reader to think or feel the same way.

Persuasive word

Everyone <u>should</u> read <u>folktales because they teach lessons.</u> One lesson in "Jack and the Beanstalk" is do not take things that are not yours. Everyone can follow that lesson in their own life.

Opinion

What's the Lesson?

COLLABORATE A folktale often has a moral, or lesson. Readers can make a personal connection to the moral. Write details about the folktale you listened to or watched.

1. _____

2. _____

3. _____

COLLABORATE Look at your notes. Circle the details you connect with the most. Talk about the lesson of the folktale with a partner. Do you agree with your partner about the lesson of the folktale? Why or why not?

Show It!

You can add a picture to help readers better understand the folktale you are writing about.

COLLABORATE Write a sentence telling your favorite part of the folktale.

My favorite part is

COLLABORATE With a partner, make a drawing to show your favorite part.

Revise

COLLABORATE Read your opinion text to a partner.

> **Did you check your**
>
> opinion?   yes   no
>
> reasons?   yes   no
>
> persuasive
> words?   yes   no

Did you give reasons that will persuade readers?

Edit

COLLABORATE Read your opinion text again.

> **Check for**
>
> ☐ subject-verb agreement
>
> ☐ singular and plural nouns
>
> ☐ common and proper nouns

Share

COLLABORATE There are many ways to present, or share, results. Make sure you use a way that is appropriate. Now choose a way to present your text and drawing.

- Read your text aloud.

- Display your work for others to read.

- Show a video of a folktale with your writing.

Reflect

MY TURN Complete the sentences.

One thing I like about my drawing is

_____

_____

_____

_____

One thing I learned about folktales is

_____

_____

_____

_____

Reflect on Your Goals

Look back at your unit goals. Use a different color to rate yourself again.

MY TURN Complete the sentences.

Reflect on Your Reading

The text from this unit that I would read again is

_____

_____

_____

Reflect on Writing

One thing I like about writing poetry is

_____

_____

_____

How to Use a Picture Dictionary

You can use a picture dictionary to find words. The words are grouped into topics. The topic of this picture dictionary is **actions**. Look at the pictures, and try to read the words. The pictures will help you understand the meanings of the words.

This is a picture of the word.

This is the word you are learning.

run

TURN and TALK Find the word **pull** in the picture dictionary. Use the picture to tell what the word means.

Actions

hide

carry

pull

bake

climb

eat

sing

How to Use a Glossary

A glossary can help you find the meanings of words you do not know. The words in a glossary are in alphabetical, or ABC, order. Guide words at the top of the pages can help you find words. They are the first and last words on the page.

> The word is in dark type.

Dd   **draw** When you **draw**, you make a picture with a writing tool.

> All words that begin with the letter **D** will be after **Dd**.

> This sentence will help you understand what the word means.

MY TURN Find the word **surprised** in the glossary. Draw a picture to help you understand what the word means.

Aa

angry When someone is **angry**, he or she is upset.

Bb

begged If you **begged**, you asked for something you needed or wanted in an emotional way.

Cc

carefully **Carefully** means in a careful way.

concentrate When you **concentrate** on something, you are paying close attention to it.

create When you **create** something, you make it.

decorate • fairly

Dd

decorate When you **decorate** something, you add things to it to make it beautiful.

doodle When you **doodle**, you draw or make marks in a random way.

draw When you **draw**, you make a picture with a writing tool.

Ee

exactly **Exactly** means in an exact, or accurate, way.

Ff

fairly **Fairly** means in a fair, or equal, way.

Gg

gathered If you **gathered** things, you chose and collected them.

Hh

happy If someone is **happy**, he or she is pleased or glad.

Ii

imagine When you **imagine**, you make a picture or idea in your mind.

Ll

learn When you **learn**, you gain knowledge.

possible • sad

Pp

possible If something is **possible**, it is able to be done.

prepared If you **prepared** for something, you got ready for it.

Rr

remember If you **remember** something, you think of it again.

Ss

sad A **sad** person is not happy.

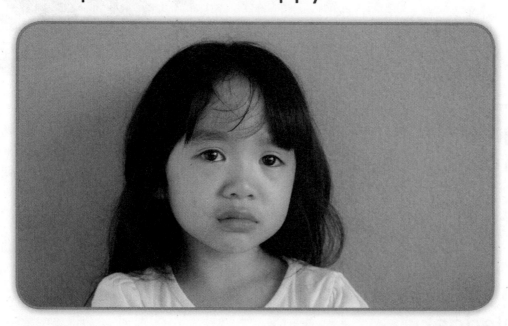

sadly **Sadly** means in a sad way.

scribble If you **scribble**, you quickly make lines and shapes in no particular way.

stored If someone **stored** something, he or she put it away for later use.

suppose When you **suppose**, you think or believe something to be true or possible.

surprised When you are **surprised**, you are having the feeling that people get when something unexpected happens.

Tt

think When you **think**, you use your mind to form ideas.

CREDITS

Text

August House Publishers, Inc.
The Clever Monkey by Rob Cleveland & Baird Hoffmire. Copyright ©2006 by Rob Cleveland and Baird Hoffmire. Reprinted by permission of August House, Inc. and Marian Reiner on their behalf.

Cricket Media
"Poodle Doodles" by Jean Hansen-Novak in *Ladybug, Ladybug and Other Favorite Poems*. Used with permission from Cricket Media; "The Box" by Sharon Wooding in *Ladybug, Ladybug and Other Favorite Poems*. Used with permission from Cricket Media; "Sandcastle" by Carol A. Grund in *Ladybug, Ladybug and Other Favorite Poems*. Used with permission from Cricket Media.

Photographs

Photo locators denoted as follows Top (T), Center (C), Bottom (B), Left (L), Right (R), Background (Bkgd)

5 Caiaimage/Robert Daly/OJO+/Getty Images, KPG_Payless/Shutterstock; **6** (Bkgd) Jamesteohart/Shutterstock, (BL) Holbox/Shutterstock; **7** Caiaimage/Robert Daly/OJO+/Getty Images, KPG_Payless/Shutterstock; **11** Photographee/Shutterstock; **12** (Bkgd) Sdecoret/Shutterstock, (C) Shimon Bar/Shutterstock, (T) Foxaon1987/Shutterstock; **13** (B) Butterfly Hunter/Shutterstock, (T) Cynthia Kidwell/Shutterstock; **14** (TCR) GUDKOV ANDREY/Shutterstock, (TR) Bloom Design/Shutterstock, (TCR) DenisNata/Shutterstock, (TL) Nikshor/Shutterstock; **15** (BL) Elenovsky/Shutterstock, (CL) GUDKOV ANDREY/Shutterstock, (BCL) Bloom Design/Shutterstock; **17** (R) Bergamont/Shutterstock, (C) Sergiy Kuzmin/Shutterstock, (L) Umberto Shtanzman/Shutterstock; **56** (C) 123RF, (L) MaxyM/Shutterstock, (R) Coprid/123RF; **58** (C) Bloom Design/Shutterstock, (CL) Ewelina Wachala/Shutterstock, (TC) 123bogdan/123RF, (TL) PixieMe/Shutterstock; **59** (C) Koosen/Shutterstock, (L) Mimadeo/Shutterstock, (R) Sidneydealmeida/Shutterstock; **68** Used with permission from August House Publishers, Inc.; **102** Daxiao Productions/Shutterstock; **104** PhotographyByMK/Shutterstock; **106** (B) Historical/Getty Images; **107** (L) Vadim Sadovski/123RF, (R) NASA; **108** (C) Berents/Shutterstock, (L) PixieMe/Shutterstock, (R) Bekshon/Shutterstock; **110** (TL) PROmax3D/Shutterstock, (CR) Ivaschenko Roman/Shutterstock, (CL) Bergamont/Shutterstock, (TR) Poter_N/Shutterstock; **111** (L) 123RF,

(C) Kamenetskiy Konstantin/Shutterstock, (R) Carroteater/Shutterstock; **138** (BL) Adisa/Shutterstock, (BR) Wolkenengel565/Shutterstock, (CL) Gerald Bernard/Shutterstock, (CR) 123RF; **140** (BL) Vslp/123RF, (CR) Sudowoodo/123RF, (TL) Itana/123RF; **141** Elenabsl/123RF; **142** (C) Eric Isselee/Shutterstock, (L) Irin-k/Shutterstock, (R) Serg64/Shutterstock; **143** (L) Midosemsem/123RF, (R) Perfect Illusion/Shutterstock; **145** (C) 123RF, (L) Evgenia Tiplyashina/Fotolia, (R) Shutterstock; **147** (L) Stefan1234/123RF, (R) AGorohov/Shutterstock; **176** (TR) stokkete/123RF, (CR) Goddard on the Go/Alamy Stock Photo, (BL) Yevhen Holovash/123RF, (CL) Yang MingQi/123RF; **177** (Bkgd) Liliia Rudchenko/123RF, (BR) Tashka/123RF, (TCR) Number168/123 RF, (TR) Evgeniy Zakharov/123RF; **178** (C) Eric Isselee/Shutterstock, (L) Ekaterina Naymushina/Shutterstock, (R) Natali_North/Shutterstock; **179** (L) Anneka/Shutterstock, (R) Jag_cz/Shutterstock; **180** Brenda Carson/Shutterstock; **181** (C) RTimages/Shutterstock, (L) Eric Isselee/Shutterstock, (R) RTimages/Shutterstock; **191** (B) Caiaimage/Robert Daly/OJO+/Getty Images, (TL) KPG_Payless/Shutterstock; **192** (C) Anderson Ross/Blend Images/Alamy Stock Photo, (T) JDC/Corbis/Getty Images; **193** Studio.G photography/Shutterstock; **194** Asiseeit/E+/Getty Images; **195** Big Cheese Photo/Getty Images; **196** Ian Allenden/123RF; **197** Damircudic/E+/Getty Images; **198** Hero Images Inc./Alamy Stock Photo; **199** (L) KidStock/Blend Images/Getty Images, (R) Jamie Grill/Tetra Images/Alamy Stock Photo; **213** (CR) Caiaimage/Robert Daly/OJO+/Getty Images, (CR) KPG_Payless/Shutterstock, (B) Multipedia/Shutterstock; **214** (C) 123RF, (L) Eric Isselee/Shutterstock, (R) 123RF; **216** (BR) MTaira/Shutterstock, (CR) Paul Brennan/Shutterstock, (TL) Africa Studio/Shutterstock, (TR) Horatiu Bota/Shutterstock; **218** (L) Design56/Shutterstock, (R) Henk Bentlage/Shutterstock; **226** Multipedia/Shutterstock; **229** Welburnstuart/Shutterstock; **239** JDC/Corbis/Getty Images; **240** Asiseeit/E+/Getty Images; **241** ESB Professional/Shutterstock; **242** Toey Toey/Shutterstock.

Illustrations

Unit 3: 21–23 Lorian Dean; **25, 67, 119, 153, 189, 232** Ken Bowser; **27–41** Sara Rojo; **54–55** Michael Slack; **63–65** Gabriel Alboroso; **69–93** Baird Hoffmire; **103** Peter Benson; **115–117** Sofia Cardoso; **122** Matt Smith; **124–125** Lynne Cravath; **126–127** John Sandford; **149–151** Nomar Perez; **155–163** Kasia Nowowiejska; **184–187** Nancy Poydar; **222–225** Juliana Motzko; **236–237** Jenny B. Harris